A Beautiful Journey

Part 1:

Journaling to Healing. . . . . .

The Beauty who owns this is:

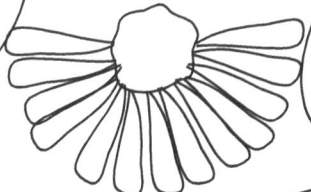

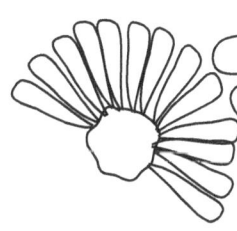

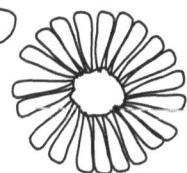

Copyright

Published by Caldwell Publishing Company
For more information, see www.Shariseantionette.com

Note You may share content in an appropriate setting exclusive to a learning environment, like bible-study, classroom, library, small group discussion, bookclub, etc.

When shared on social media please tag us and feel free to use any combination of hashtags:

> IG: @ShariseAntionette
> FB: @MyBeautifulBookBoss
> #MyBeautifulBookBoss
> #MBBB
> #ABeautifulJourney
> #StayBeautifulBeWise

ISBN: 978-1-956318-19-7 Black and white
ISBN: 978-1-956318-21-0 Colored interior

How To Use this Journal

A Beautiful Journey is the companion Journal to 'A Heart for the Home" memoir. This journal was created to go alongside the same flow, structure, mood, and principles as the book. However, the journal can be used with or without the book.

**If you have both together, great! You can read the book and follow along in your journal at the same time.

**If you only have this journal, wonderful! You can follow each day according to the directions below and be willing to do the heart work to get the transformation you desire, just as the author in her own true story!

This journal includes a daily prompt that coincides with each chapter in its companion novel (A Heart for the Home). ** You can choose to complete each prompt daily or weekly!**

Each daily prompt is divided into four categories; Statement, Explanation, Action, Go Deeper. Each section is labeled to make it easier to follow. Here is the set-up example below.

The very first page as well as the very last page, to begin this journal, has the same structure but different exercises then the rest of our daily prompts.

**optional

Structure of Journal

Daily Set-Up: Section numbers and Title
        (This is part 1 of the 3 part series, section Childhood.)

Chapter and Day (the chapter and the day will always have the same number.) You can do a page everyday or you can extend the lesson by weeks. Chapter 1 Day 1 can be done all in one full day or spread out for the week. If you're doing weeks, think of it as Chapter 1 Week 1 instead of Day 1.

Statement-A paragraph from, 'A Heart for The Home' with the page number.

Explanation-This is our focus point for the day. Some days is just one point and other days there are multiple.

Action- I give you questions to answer, thoughts to think about, or mini exercises to do! You are more than welcome to add your own additional task.
        *For example- If something I said made you think of making a phone call to a loved one, then by all means do that act of kindness and journal it as well!

Go Deeper-We want to find the problem but solve it at the root. Roots go deep so we will too!

Table of Contents

Section I: Childhood

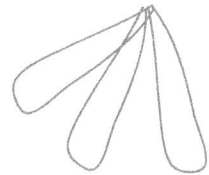

A Beautiful Journey

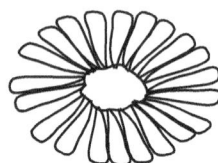

Is the companion journal to *A Heart for the Home Series*. If you haven't ordered your copy, be sure to get one soon.

All concepts are coming from the book. This journal was created as a complementary source to enhance the reader's experience as well as extend an offer to go along the same journey beside the author.

Do you have to have both in order to reap the benefits? No you do not have to have them both. You will still get the main idea and hopefully permission to allow healing to take place in your heart! These resources were created for you to become your better self.

At MBBB, we are all about self-identity, alignment and clarity. We desire for you to be Happy, Healthy, and Whole. We are committed to creating unique products to continue to serve our audience in hopes that you actually receive breakthroughs, transformations, and finally have a place to grow, thrive, and be all that God created you to be!

We are so glad you are here with us and we WELCOME you to My Beautiful Book Boss The Movement. To learn more about us listen to the Podcast, visit the website, or contact us directly.

Stay Beautiful, Be Wise, and Be All that God Created you to be!

Thankyou,
Sharise Antionette

Pretend you are this flower.

Somewhere along the way you lost your vibrant colors, shedding some petals, and have become delicate, fragile and vulnerable. You are NOT weak, just in a state that now your sisters can help lift you up!

This journal is packed with challenges to help you dig deep within, put away excuse, face your fears, and heal from past pains.

You have to trust me on this journey to a better you. Our promise is to uncover the truth by exposing the lies, connect with your feminine self to fully express her with personality, and become your own boss without losing yourself, creating balance without compromise, and honoring God.

Let's Begin!

Color Me Beautiful!

Sample coloring page from "Color Me Beautiful" A Healing Coloring Book! Available on Amazon NOW!

Ch.1   Day 1/ Week 1

STATEMENT:

"Now before you say "Aww! She's an angel." These recollections are only from what I was told and not from my own perspective. I want you to relate to my whole experience to fully understand the entire story." (Excerpt from *A Heart for the Home*, pg. 11).

EXPLANATION:

As mentioned above, a lot of my past memories have the influence of others because these thoughts were told to me and are not necessarily true memories of my own. It can be good or bad depending on if the perspective was in fact the truth or a misunderstood version coming from the person telling the story.

ACTION:

Today I want you to take some time to think about your memories. Write as many as you can down, then answer the following questions for each memory. Are they just your memories? Or were they told to you from another person's perspective? How does this truth change your perception?

GO DEEPER:

If you have Memories that you struggle with because they come from someone else's point of view. I want you to release those feelings, emotions, and attachments tied to the other person's beliefs. You do not have to have the same reaction, experience, or outcome as the people around you.

_____

_____

_____

_____

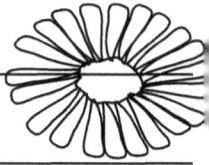

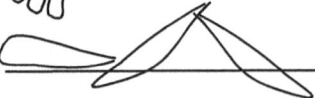

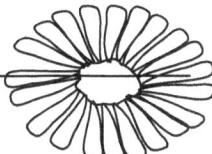

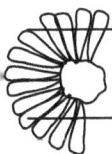
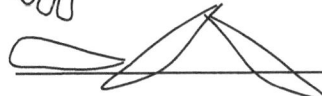
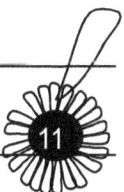

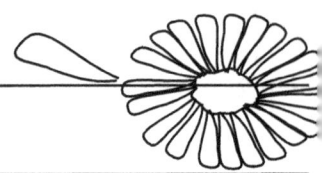

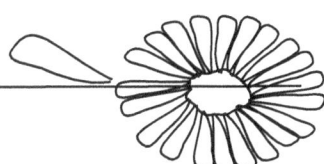

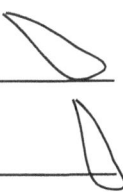

STATEMENT:

"I may not have recognized how special she truly was to us. I may not have recognized that her job as grandma, mother, friend, and caregiver was extremely important. In fact, if she wasn't selfless and made herself available, so many people would have been left stranded, helpless, and without provision, including us" (Excerpt from *A Heart for the Home*, pg. 14).

EXPLANATION:

It wouldn't be until I became an adult that I started to realize the many missed opportunities to learn from my elders. Even though they were my relatives, school teachers, or church leaders, there was so much wisdom they had to share. I wish I would have slowed down and enjoyed the time I had with them.

I was a product of a lack of information, and you could really tell from the choices I made in my youth. I often misunderstood the adults around me. I didn't know the depths of becoming an adult nor did I understand the important positions, titles, and responsibilities they held.

Most of the time, I could only see them as teacher, janitor, Mom, Dad, Grandma, uncle, aunt, bus driver, etc. Now I get to shine light on my job title as stay-at-home mom, homeschooler, housewife, and mompreneur.

ACTION:

Take a trip down memory lane with me and think about one person (or people) who truly impacted your life. If you are struggling to find positive memories, really consider the person you are becoming now. Did that significant other have any minor role in your evolving (whether that person was nice or mean)?

GO DEEPER:

I gave myself the title of Biblical Femininity Coach to other Housewives / SAHM's. What title seems so insignificant you can turn into a Bold Beautiful Boss title? Write it down, and say it aloud proudly.

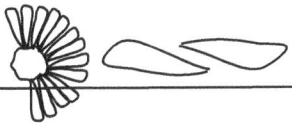
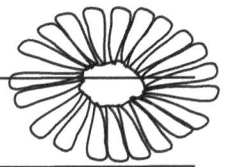

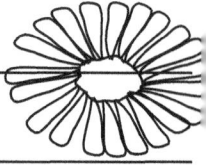

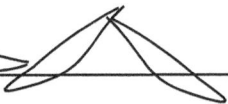

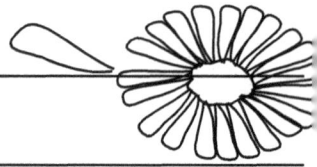

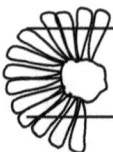

Statement

"Oddly enough, mimicking the tv turned into desiring the same lives I admired. Young teens were often depicted in immature relationships, money, fame, sex, drugs, and alcohol. This list is what my heart desperately hoped for" (Excerpt from *A Heart for the Home*, pg. 17).

Explanation:

I'm sure we have all had dreams and aspirations as children. I remember being asked, "What do you want to be when you grow up?" I would always have a long list of careers, jobs, and interests. This list as a child turned into hobbies as a young adult, which led to many years of being confused about the gifts I possessed because of the term "multi-passionate."

There was one that seemed to stand out more than the rest, dance! I didn't get to pursue my life long dream of being a dancer. However, I had no idea the many interests from my past would play such a dominant role in my life now.

I'm so thankful I did not have a career in dance when I was a teenager because I would have become a backup dancer for entertainment. I would have done things I would not have been proud of and would have been willing to degrade my image for popularity, passion and fame. Now I can use the love I have for art and teaching to positively impact the world while still maintaining holiness before God.

Action:

What are some things you dreamed of doing as a child? Did you grow up and become that? Are there some things you wanted to be that were influenced by outside sources like: media, school, neighbors, family, friends, etc?

Go Deeper:

There's nothing wrong with dance, music, or anything other than becoming a preacher, singing in the choir, or praise dancing. It's only wrong when it is immodest, sinful, and lusty behavior. I can use dance, and you can use whatever God has given you to do to display His righteous character. Write down a talent you thought was wrong or bad because it didn't necessarily fit in the church culture.

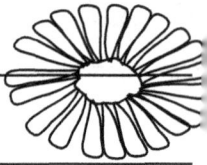

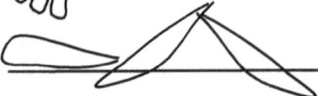
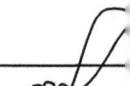

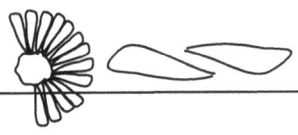
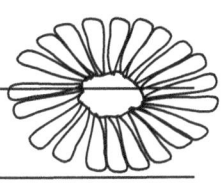
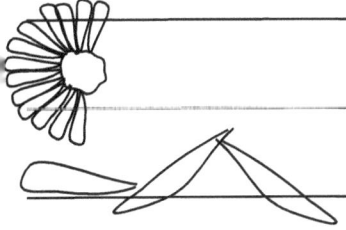

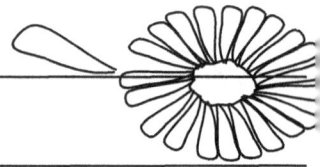

STATEMENT

"I really needed someone to sit me down and say, "Sharise, you don't have all the answers. You are not alone. Your family does love you. Have you considered their perspective other than your own point of view? What about your mom? Dad? Sister? Brother? Don't they love you and care about you?" (Excerpt from *A Heart for the Home*, pg. 21-22)

EXPLANATION:

Have you ever heard of the saying *the small fox spoils the whole vine?* Or *It only takes one bad fruit to spoil the whole bunch? You strain at the gnat but swallow the whole camel?* Well, these saying are basically stating sometimes we can make the little things into something larger, unnecessary, and elevate them higher than the most important thing at that time.

They are often overemphasized, over-exaggerated, imaginative thoughts, not reality, just real to the person having the experience. I'm not saying your encounter wasn't true. I'm suggesting we take these thoughts, feelings, and uncertain emotions before the Word of God to check them. We need to make sure we didn't take something out of context and see if it really happened instead of going by our feelings, thoughts, or what we think we saw or heard.

That was so me as a child. I really did not have a mature understanding. I was very curious but missing a lot of important, meaningful information. After losing trust in people, I often jumped to the conclusion, misunderstood the situation, and judged before having all of the info. It led to a lot of assumptions. I heavily depended on the TV or school for my answers in life. I often felt isolated from my family because I could not express that I needed someone to talk honestly to me not as a five year old or eight year old but as a person who can understand and make intelligent decisions if given a chance.

ACTION:

Have you moved in fear, anxiety, or with haste because of your own insecurities? Write down your insecurities and name them. Speak them out loud and say you are no longer insecure or held back by those fears. Afterward, cross them out and write your new Powerful Positive Proclamations!

CONTINUE TO NEXT PAGE.........

I am no longer anxious, jittery, or trying to figure out things on my own. I will only wait for clear instructions from the Lord. When things don't work out I still trust Him anyway! I do not move in fear. I move in FAITH.

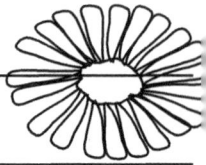

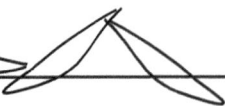

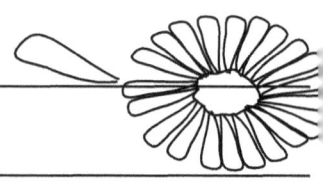

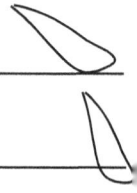

STATEMENT

"We are born into families for a reason. Parents, children, adults and youth,we all have our own place because we all have unique gifts and talents even at those stages in life that if used properly will be a blessing and the answer to solve each other's problems" (Excerpt from *A Heart for the Home*, pg. 24).

EXPLANATION:

My family respected each other, young and old, and taught us to respect one another too. Unfortunately, I see so many children treated as lesser because of their age and for me it became one of the main reasons why I didn't trust adults as much.

My parents didn't just encourage me to follow my dreams but to plan out how to get there using wisdom. They advised me to go to college and earn a degree in a field that will generate lots of money. It is what their generation did successfully.

The career that I desired as a dancer was very risky because of the stigmatism as a "starving artist." They told me to have a back-up plan. At that time I was offended by their suggestion and thought they weren't being supportive. Now that I am an adult I am able to follow my dreams plus use wisdom and still get the desired results. I get to be who God created me to be from the beginning, doing what I love to do, and making a solid income.

ACTION:

How were you treated as a child and how did this treatment affect you? Do you think family is important? What are some healthy boundaries for family and non family members? Are you doing what you love to do now? Why or why not? Have you become who God originally created you to be? Or are you still finding out who you were destined to be? Why or why not?

CONTINUE TO NEXT PAGE . . . .

Go Deeper:

I served as a housewife for nine years and as a homeschool mom for eight years without pay. This was a life of sacrifice I was willing to make to better my family and obey the call. God has used these experiences to prepare and now has positioned me as an author, podcast producer, book designer and housewife coach. What experiences has led you to the calling on your life. Think about every scenario that applies even if it was voluntary, unpaid, short-term, etc.

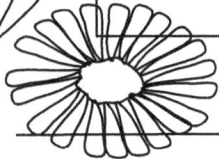

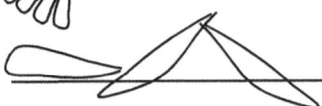

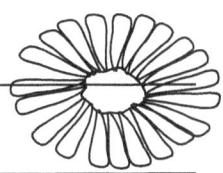

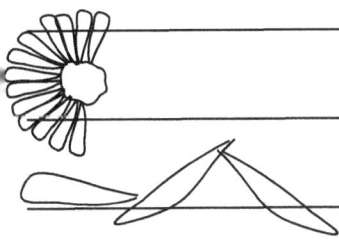

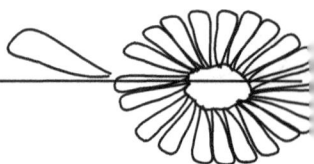

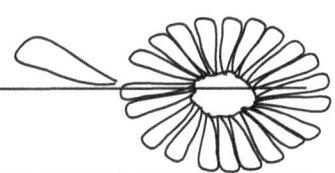

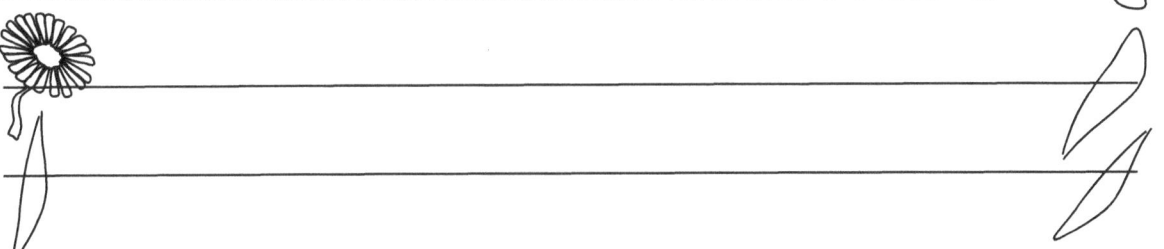
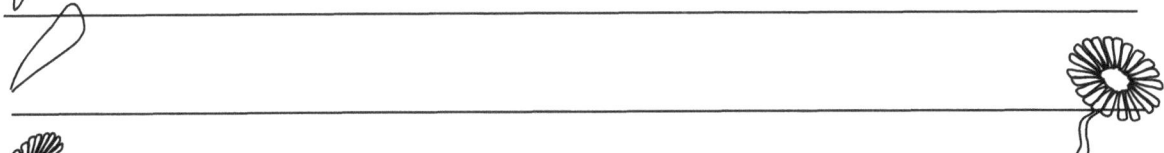

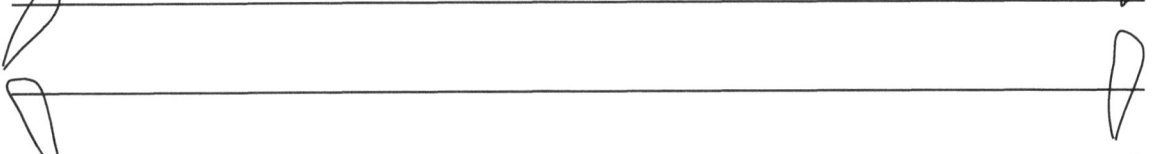
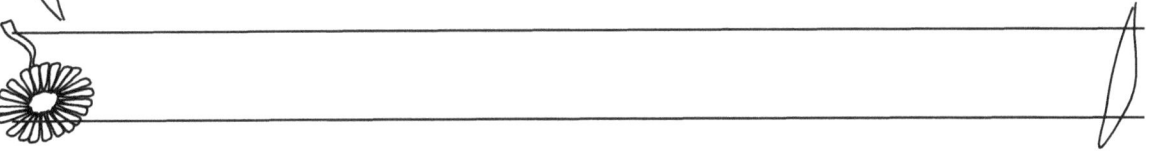
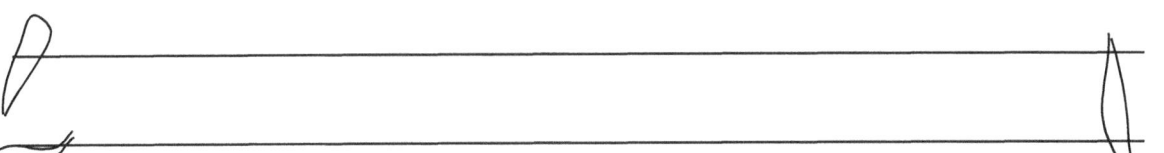

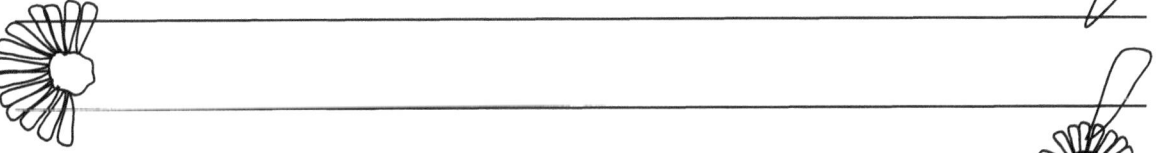
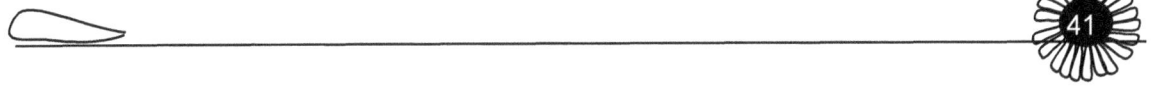

STATEMENT

"I really didn't have responsibility in my home, so I grew up thinking everything would be handed to me and everyone was at my disposal. Respect your elders little girl" (Excerpt from *A Heart for the Home*, pg. 26).

EXPLANATION:

Today I want to mention one unavoidable thing that happens in life, change. Everything living on this earth at some point will undergo change. No matter if it's big or small, or barely noticeable. Change, growth, and maturity is inevitable unless something stops it from happening.

Change is supposed to happen to us all, but things can prevent us from evolving or maturing, like, early death, diseases, illnesses, trauma, etc. In the chapter I quoted above, my main point was that children grow into adults, so we can't dismiss children because of their age or treat them like they are ignorant. Why? The bigger picture is that dumb, worthless, can't do anything right little child will grow into a self-conscious, angry, vengeful adult.

It is not always the case, especially when an intervention happens from a parent, school teacher, peer, or God himself. There are things in my past that greatly altered my future in a negative way. I've seen so many mean people mistreat other people, including innocent children, because they themselves are defending the broken little child inside of them.

ACTION:

Take a deep breath before we begin. Are there any past memories coming up as we went through today's discussion? If so, write them down in as much detail as possible. What came up? Why did that bother you? Did you know it was still a problem? What else could be hindering you from healing in this particular area? Below will be some ways to let this go from your heart, from your mind, and from your own expectations. Take some time to think and ultimately do what's best for you!

CONTINUE TO NEXT PAGE . . . .

Stress Relieving Ideas: * take a warm bath but make it luxurious by adding bath salt, bubbles, and flower petals, as you meditate, listen to music, or read a book * Create a small corner to decorate as your safe space to come to *Light a candle or use essential oils to make the house smell cheerful and fantastic * pray for your heart to heal * do art, color, paint, draw, etc.

_____

_____

_____

_____

_____

_____

_____

_____

_____

_____

_____

_____

_____

_____

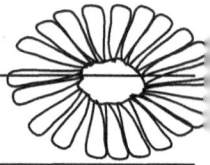

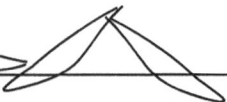

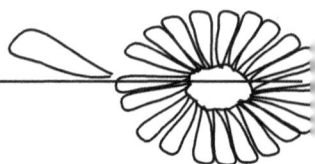

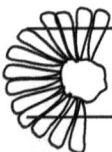

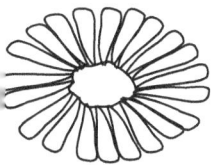

Section 1: ChildHood

Ch.7   Day 7/Week 7

STATEMENT

"I have to say, looking back, I caused a lot of conflict in my own relationships. I had a smart mouth, would act in self-defense, and was always ready to prove a point" (Excerpt from *A Heart for the Home*, pg. 29).

EXPLANATION:

There are so many different angles I can attack this subject. I want to point out two main things. *A lack of* information and *wrongful* information. We can only make decisions based upon what we know. Let's break down this topic a little more.

Lots of information is passed back and forth throughout our day to day busy, hectic lives. We turn on the news to get our weather and latest reports. We ask the teachers what our children are doing in school. Higher management passes down our to-do list for the day. If we go out to eat, the waitress or checkout counter is giving us our food that we ordered. Back and forth emails from clients. Voice messages from missed phone calls.

There is one common thread out of all of these scenarios and that is an **in-between person**. Because so many people are involved, information is easily misunderstood, messed up, and taken out of context. This is exactly what happened when I was a child. So many people were saying so many different things and I was at the blame of it all.

This led to a lot of anger, bitterness, and resentment. Which leads me to my next point. I was upset because of a lack of information on my part. I didn't know life was this way. I could only see it from my little girl's eyes. I assumed because I was sweet, honest, and genuine, that everyone else would follow the same direction.

You can't hold on to negative feelings because of what someone else did. And you can't blame yourself for the things that you did. It's time to take healing into our own hands and forgive!

ACTION:

Have you ever had to admit you were wrong? Let's take a look at some of the things that we may have done, whether we meant to or not. What are some mistakes that we have made that we can change now? What could you have done differently? Who and what will you forgive?

CONTINUE TO NEXT PAGE . . . .

Is there any situation you had a lack of information and made a judgement? What happened? What would you have done differently? Is there any situation you had a wrongful information and made a judgement? What happened? What would you have done differently?

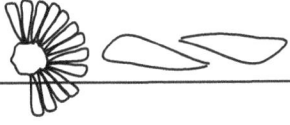
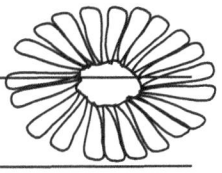

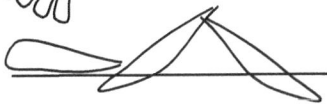

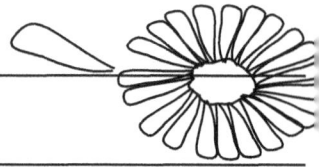

STATEMENT

"My parents would leave for work while we were asleep, and come back home just in time to fix dinner and head to bed. They supported each of us in pursuing our interests. My sister was a cross-country champion. My brother had a natural talent for gymnastics. And then there was me" (Excerpt from *A Heart for the Home*, pg. 31).

EXPLANATION:

The classic Ugly Duckling story right here. I can skip over the explanation and jump right into the action step. I will say this about feeling like the black sheep in my family. 1) I'm not sure many people knew I actually felt this way. 2) I don't know if anyone saw themselves as really tormenting me. 3) I don't know if anyone recognizes the power of their own words. 4) I'm not sure I knew I was experiencing trauma.

I went through my younger years defending myself, rebelling against authority, and trying to prove a point. Eventually, I tired myself out and became weary, fearful, and hopeless. I walked around with so much weight on my shoulders feeling like I could never share the pain I have experienced or the frustrations I was having as an adult. We are supposed to have it all together right? It was just something minor. Get over it. WRONG.

ACTION:

What past incidents have you dismissed or been told to forget about because it's not that serious? How has this situation affected you? Is it in fact a big deal or a small problem? Do you need help overcoming this situation your life? Have you considered therapy, coaching, or some other form of healing? If you have, did it help? What do you need to move forward?

CONTINUE TO NEXT PAGE . . . .

Being able to identify trauma and face it head on is a major key to healing. Digging deeper until you can't find anymore questions to answer is the secret to uncovering the whole truth and finding the root to the problem. How close to healing are you?

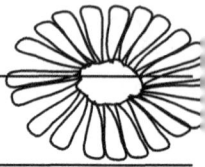

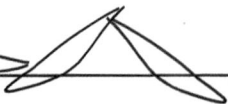

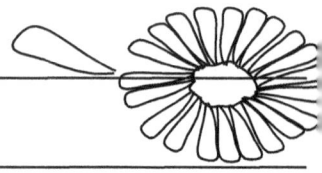

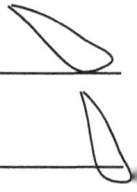

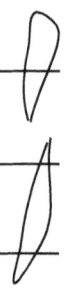

STATEMENT

"There is no age requirement to start teaching healthy habits, establishing clear rules, and keeping godly boundaries. The sooner you instill values inside of your children the better. There is a time where the grace of teaching them your principles will come to an end" (Excerpt from *A Heart for the Home*, pg. 34).

EXPLANATION:

When taking a trip there is a checklist we all follow. Maybe we start the process by noting all of the things we need to complete before leaving. Also, purchasing final items beforehand, so we can pack them all up before the time of departing. Another must-do task is possibly getting a pet sitter or someone to cover for us at work.

My point is that there are things we need to do before taking a journey. Let's apply this process to ourselves. I didn't realize the many misconceptions and misinformation I had from childhood because of a lack of really raw talks about life. It was also due to a lack of listening, obedience, or believing in my parents.

A checklist for life: *Be a whole person *Know yourself *Develop and mature as a person *Learn how to love people * Master kindness and grace with own family *Use gifts and talents to bring self joy *Be a blessings to the earth *Teach someone else your wisdom *Make sure your soul is healthy, healed, and free from chains. *Know who you are as a person
*Develop a healthy personality

ACTION:

Is there a time you took a situation out of context based upon your limited perception? If so, write it the way you mistakenly thought it was. Now rewrite it with the knowledge you have now. Rewrite it the way God would. Compare the similarities and differences.

CONTINUE TO NEXT PAGE . . . .

Create your own checklist for the current season you are in. You can write what you have, what you need, and what you desire. If you want to go a little deeper, ask yourself why you wrote these things on the checklist for life. Can you add any emergency items on your list? What's your reason for having these things in case of an emergency?

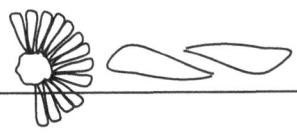
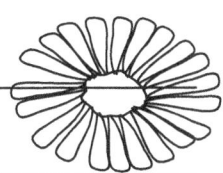

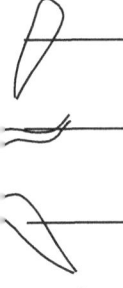

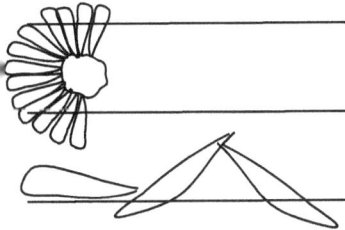

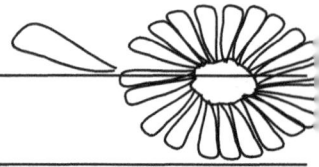

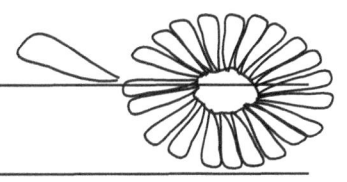

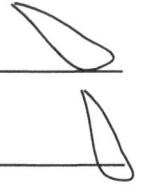

STATEMENT

"Sometimes I felt bad for the harsh feelings I actually had against my own house and then I remembered how I tried to do as I was told, but for some odd reason, Sharise was the blame for it all.." (Insert from A Heart for the Home pg 41)

EXPLANATION:

It is so natural to feel like our opinion is right all the time. One of the hardest things I have had to confront about myself is when I feel like I have to speak my mind.

I feel like if I don't say something, then the other person will continue to mistreat me or have the wrong answer to the problem and won't be able to figure it out without me.

This type of thinking screams a lack of trust somewhere deep in the heart. You may not have even thought about it like this until now. I have realized on this journey to healing, that I developed serious trust issues to the point it would have crippled the future and success the Lord had planned for my life.

You have to have trust in your faith, relationships, business, homeschooling, when trying something new, so on and so forth. Having trust doesn't mean you won't feel the fear. Having trust means that even though you have no idea how things are going to work out, you choose to believe it will all come together.

Trust is one of the main reasons I created *A Beautiful Heart Affirmation Cards* and *Becoming More Beautiful coaching program* for women who desire to deepen their relationships, build a business, impact their families, while being confident with herself (Check page 98 for more info).

ACTION:

What came up for you when you read this journal entry? Why do you think this was brought to your attention? Have you felt like this before? Do you have a plan to work on this particular area? Do a comparison between what happens when this challenge is under control versus when you are battling against it, what are some of the positive and negative effects that occur?

GO DEEPER:

What does trust mean to you? How would you define trust in your relationships, business, faith, and with yourself?

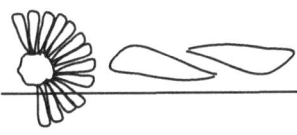
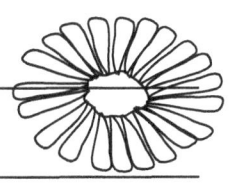

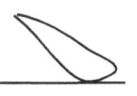

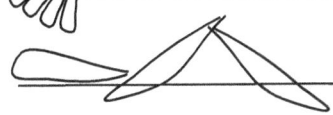

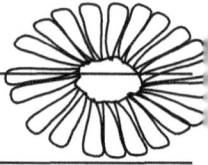

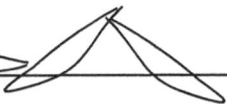

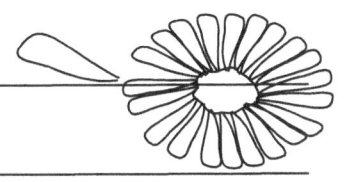

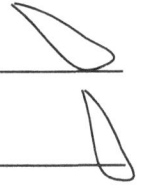

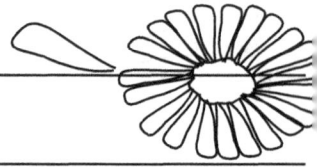

Statement

"With all of their effort, the love they provided was inundated by outside influences penetrating into the walls of our home by attaching its ideologies on the people who lived in the house.." (Insert from A Heart for the Home pg 41)

Explanation:

Life is a journey, and I am so glad we are in this process of healing, growth, and prosperity. A part of it is self-growth and self-discovery. Sometimes we don't take into consideration the things we learned growing up. I am speaking from the age of 20 and under. All of the pieces are one big puzzle.

If we aren't careful some of these old ways of thinking can follow well into our mature years. They can linger around for our entire lifetime. It doesn't matter what happened yesterday. If you have understanding, use it and make some things happen for you right now.

Action:

What are some rules, teachings, ways, or traditions from childhood that you have kept in your adulthood? What are some new things you introduced in your adulthood that didn't come from your upbringing? What are some things you didn't change that maybe you can experiment with swapping into healthier practices? If you feel you have dropped the ball a little, that's ok, write your plan out to get your life back on track!

Go Deeper:

The only thing we can change and control is ourselves. Challenge yourself during the next encounter with a situation to take a step back, process the information, ask questions for more clarity, give yourself time to make a conscious response, and then follow through with a decision.

I have been truly slowing my response and reaction down so I can better handle the problems that come up on a constant basis. Taking my time to follow these steps have been blessing me as well as the people involved in these scenarios.

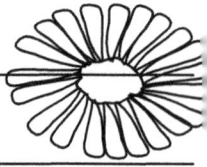

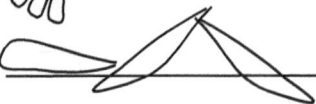

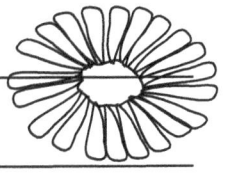

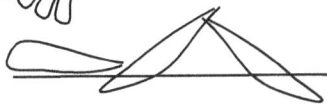

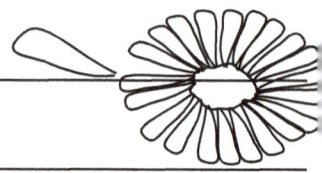

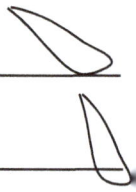

Pretend you are this flower.

CONGRATULATIONS Beautiful! I pray you have found your vibrant colors again!

This journey was full of ups, downs, twists, turns, gains, and losses. I pray you were able to let go of the things keeping you tangled up. I pray you can now move into all of the great things God has for YOU!

You have trusted me throughout this process. I hope the messages were loud and clear as an introduction to your Creator. Some things go deeper than what you can see on the surface. I created this journal for you to go deep and uncover some hidden truths.

May you continue to walk in your freedom and pass this blessing onto another beautiful Sis! You can gift this set or just tell others so they can order one too!

Stay Beautiful

Color who you are now!
Then compare this flower to the first one (at the beginning of this book.)

Additional Resources

I've created a comparison chart immediately following this page for you to have extra space to process and analyze your transformation.

I don't believe we will ever come to a stopping point of change. We should want to continue to learn new techniques, grow in our capacity to love, evolve into our better selves, and strive for excellence!

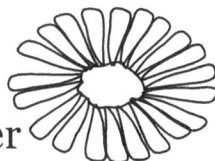

If this has truly changed your life consider starting a book club, or sharing this resource to your church, small group, school, library, community center, non-profit organization, labor and delivery at your local hospital, etc.

You are more than welcome to redo this journey as many times as you want to. The comparison charts may be copied and duplicated without restriction or limitation.

They are for you to continue to check in! They also can be applied in other areas of your life or if you go in a different direction, they should be able to come along with you!

Stay Beautiful, Be Wise, Be All that God created YOU to be!

What "lightbulb" moments have you had? Right it in the takeaways.
What are some thoughts you want to change, recognize it may be faulty, but still is in a serious battle against it? Write the answers in "Need More Time." (Do this exercise as you continue to break free from old mindsets. I've provided a few extra sheets if you need them. You also can make copies **of this sheet ONLY** just to have extra for days ahead!)

Takeaways   Need more time

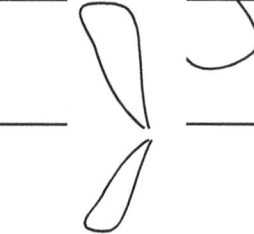

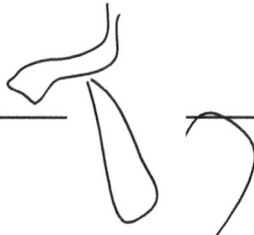

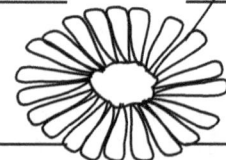

What "lightbulb" moments have you had? Right it in the takeaways.
What are some thoughts you want to change, recognize it may be faulty, but still is in a serious battle against it? Write the answers in "Need More Time." (Do this exercise as you continue to break free from old mindsets. You can make copies *of this sheet ONLY* just to have extra for days ahead!)

Takeaways   Need more time

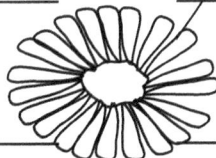

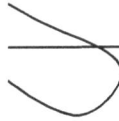

_____   _____

_____   _____

_____   _____

_____   _____

_____   _____

_____   _____

_____   _____

_____   _____

_____   _____

_____   _____

What "lightbulb" moments have you had? Right it in the takeaways.
What are some thoughts you want to change, recognize it may be faulty, but still is in a serious battle against it? Write the answers in "Need More Time." You can make copies *of this sheet ONLY* just to have extra for days ahead!)

Takeaways

Need more time

What "lightbulb" moments have you had? Right it in the takeaways.
What are some thoughts you want to change, recognize it may be faulty, but still is in a serious battle against it? Write the answers in "Need More Time." You can make copies *of this sheet ONLY* just to have extra for days ahead!)

Takeaways

Need more time

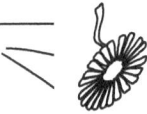

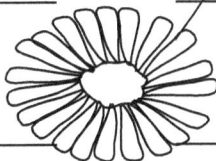

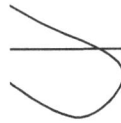

What "lightbulb" moments have you had? Right it in the takeaways.
What are some thoughts you want to change, recognize it may be faulty, but still is in a serious battle against it? Write the answers in "Need More Time." You can make copies *of this sheet ONLY* just to have extra for days ahead!)

Takeaways

Need more time

What "lightbulb" moments have you had? Right it in the takeaways.
What are some thoughts you want to change, recognize it may be faulty, but still is in a serious battle against it? Write the answers in "Need More Time." You can make copies *of this sheet ONLY* just to have extra for days ahead!)

Takeaways

Need more time

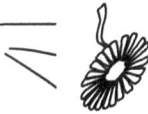

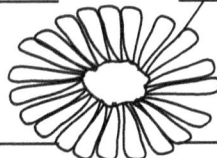

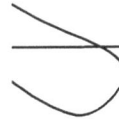

What "lightbulb" moments have you had? Right it in the takeaways.
What are some thoughts you want to change, recognize it may be faulty, but still is in a serious battle against it? Write the answers in "Need More Time." You can make copies *of this sheet ONLY* just to have extra for days ahead!)

Takeaways

Need more time

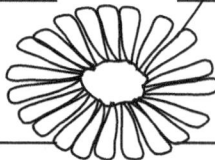

Before you Go check out more available resources!

Be sure to Listen to My Beautiful Book Boss the Podcast on your favorite streaming site. New episodes Fridays @6am EST!

Grab your freebie *4 Foundational Action Guide* located on my links page.

Like my content? Check out Sharise Caldwell YouTube

***Be the first to get exclusive deals and to know about New Products before they become available to the public, Sign-up for our email list Today!

Join our private group for Community, Commitment, Challenges, and Conversations.

Facebook.com/MyBeautifulBookBoss_TheMovement

<3 We appreciate all of your support! Please continue to Share, Like, Comment, Rate, Tag us, Leave detailed Reviews **Follow** us on our social media platforms and Subscribe if you haven't already!

IG: @ShariseAntionette FB:@MyBeautifulBookBoss

YT: Sharise Caldwell

HashTags: #MyBeautifulBookBoss #ABeautifulJourney #AHeartForTheHome #StayBeautifulBeWise #MBBB

*****TAG us in your stories so we can add you to ours*****

Get Your Book Today!
Stay Tuned for the new releases of Part II and III . . .

A Heart
for the Home

Mending every area of brokenness
in my Heart

Part I: CHILDHOOD

Sharise A. Caldwell

Check out our other amazing products on Amazon!

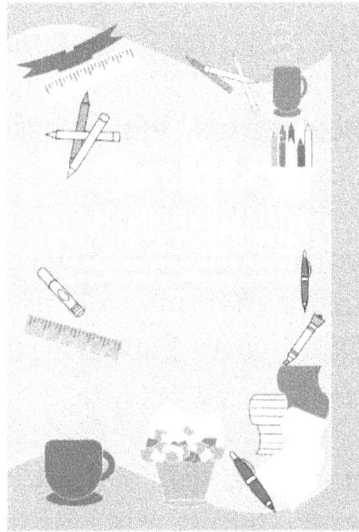

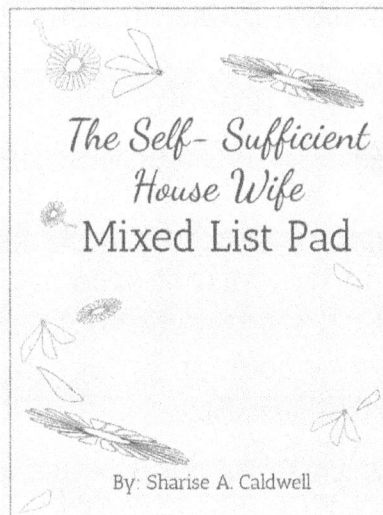

The
Self-Sufficient
House Wife
3 Month Planner System

Sharise A. Caldwell

The
Self-Sufficient
House Wife
12 Month Calendar &
Reward System

Sharise A. Caldwell

Stay
Beautiful
Scripture Notebook Journal

Sharise A. Caldwell

The Self-Sufficient
House Wife
Mixed List Pad

By: Sharise A. Caldwell

We have over 20 resources serving housewives, christian women, and homeschool families. Be sure to follow the author page on Amazon to see all new releases!

Programs & Services

We are now serving authors and course creators who would like to add a workbook, journal, or set of affirmation cards to their brand. If your content is sinful or coming directly against Christianity or Jesus Christ, you automatically do not qualify and will be politely turned down. ********This only applies to our formatting services because we will be associated with our clients brand and content.********

- ❤ Full Design, Layout, Structure, Cover Spread, and Format
- ❤ Weekly LIVE clarity meeting and updates (up to 6 weeks)
- ❤ Up to 6 changes, edits, and special request
- ❤ 1-on-1 Info meeting (Acceptance, Approval, and Qualification)
- ❤ Design interpretation within 7 days of Approval
- ❤ Careful attention to details and our client's vision
- ❤ Quick production time
- ❤ Estimation quote and time frame

Becoming More Beautiful is our signature program serving housewives who want to become homemakers. We will be discussing how to build intimacy in 4 categories of relationships; People, Your Self, Business, and Priorities, especially in the current season of your life.

- ❤ 12 week coaching program
- ❤ 12 LIVE sessions
- ❤ 12 LIVE Q & A's
- ❤ Sisterhood and Private Community
- ❤ Special Guest and Master Mentor Sessions
- ❤ Graduation Ceremony

❤❤❤❤All Programs and services may be found and applied to ONLY at our website: www.ShariseAntionette.com ❤❤❤

www.ingramcontent.com/pod-product-compliance
Lightning Source LLC
Chambersburg PA
CBHW080424030426
42335CB00020B/2571